W9-AXP-430

BROWN

By Patricia M. Stockland
Illustrated by Julia Woolf

Content Consultant
Susan Kesselring, MA
Literacy Educator and K-1 Teacher

magic wagon

(COLORS)

visit us at www.abdopublishing.com

Printed in the United States of America, North Mankato, Minnesota.
082010
012011

THIS BOOK CONTAINS AT LEAST 10% RECYCLED MATERIALS.

Text by Patricia M. Stockland
Illustrations by Julia Woolf
Edited by Nadia Higgins
Series design by Nicole Brecke
Cover and interior layout by Emily Love

Library of Congress Cataloging-in-Publication Data
Stockland, Patricia M.
  Brown / by Patricia M. Stockland ; illustrated by Julia Woolf
     p. cm. — (Colors)
  ISBN 978-1-61641-135-0
  1. Brown—Juvenile literature. 2. Colors—Juvenile literature. I. Woolf, Julia. II. Title.
  QC495.5.S7724 2011
  535.6—dc22
                            2010013988

I pack my backpack for the zoo.

My backpack is brown.

4

My brother buys tickets at the gate.

The tickets are brown.

I gaze up at a big bear.

The bear is brown.

My brother points to a nest.

The nest is brown.

A pelican flies out of the nest!

The pelican's belly is brown.

A chimpanzee smiles at me.

The chimp's face is brown.

We stop to eat some raisins.

The raisins are brown.

15

16

My brother shows me some buffalo.

The buffalo are brown.

I show my brother the giraffes.

The giraffes' spots are brown.

19

My brother gives me his cap.

The cap is brown.

What Is Brown?

There are three primary colors: red, blue, and yellow. These colors combine to create other colors. Red, blue, and yellow together will make brown.

Primary Colors

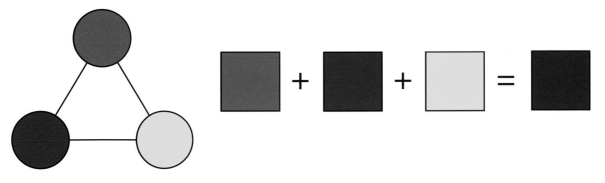

How many brown things can you find in this book?

Words to Know

buffalo—a large, shaggy animal that has hooves and horns.

gaze—to look at something for a long time.

pelican—a large bird that lives near water and scoops up fish with its long bill.

Web Sites

To learn more about the color brown, visit ABDO Group online at **www.abdopublishing.com**. Web sites about the colors are featured on our Book Links page. These links are routinely monitored and updated to provide the most current information available.